STARTERS
NATURE

Insects
You Can Find

Macdonald Educational

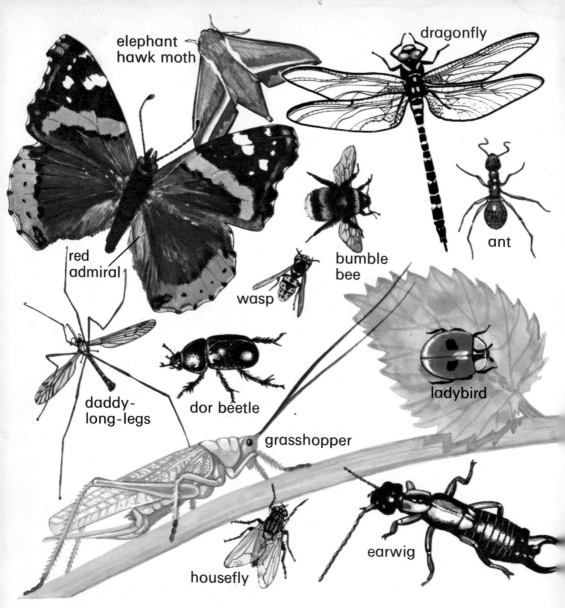

elephant hawk moth

dragonfly

bumble bee

ant

wasp

red admiral

daddy-long-legs

dor beetle

ladybird

grasshopper

housefly

earwig

All these are insects.
There are thousands of different kinds.
How many do you see here?

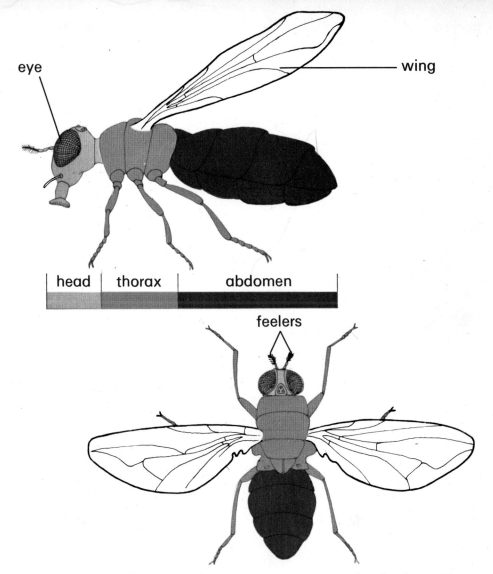

All insects have three parts to their bodies.
They all have six legs.
Most have four wings, some have two.
Just a few do not have any.

cabbage
white

red admiral

small
tortoise-shell

painted lady

Butterflies are beautiful insects.
You can often see these kinds.
They come to buddleia bushes to feed.

eggs

caterpillar

pupa

acetate

nasturtium leaves

sticky tape

water

large white butterfly

You can collect caterpillars.
Be sure to notice what they are eating.
Give them the same kind of food every day.
Watch how they change.

elephant
hawk moth

oak eggar

white ermine

buff tip

magpie
moth

blood-vein

red underwing

barred
yellow

There are very many pretty moths.
They often fly at night.
They fly towards lights.

6

dandelions

cocoon

woolly-
bear
caterpillar

garden
tiger
moth

Look for 'woolly-bear' caterpillars in spring.
Feed them on dandelion or nettle leaves.
Soon they will spin cocoons.
In summer the tiger moth comes out.

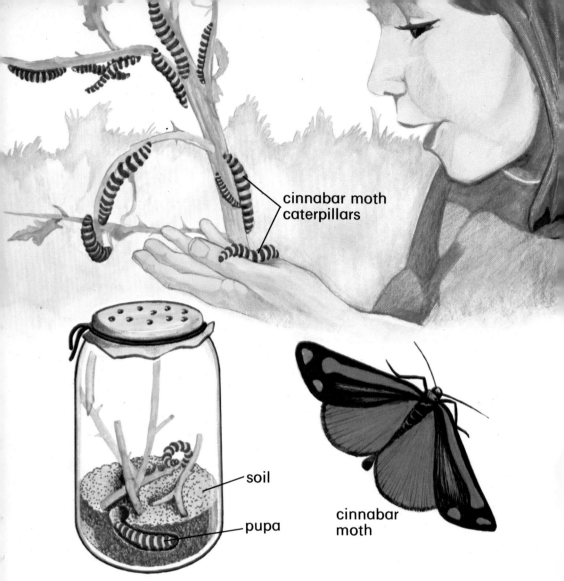

cinnabar moth caterpillars

soil

pupa

cinnabar moth

You can find this caterpillar in June.
It eats ragwort and groundsel leaves.
It goes into the soil to change to a pupa.
The moth hatches after the winter.

8

pupa

pupae

small glass or
plastic jar

plastic
margarine pot

Collect soil from under bushes.
Look for moth pupae in it.
Keep them in a pot of slightly damp soil.
Watch for the moths to hatch.

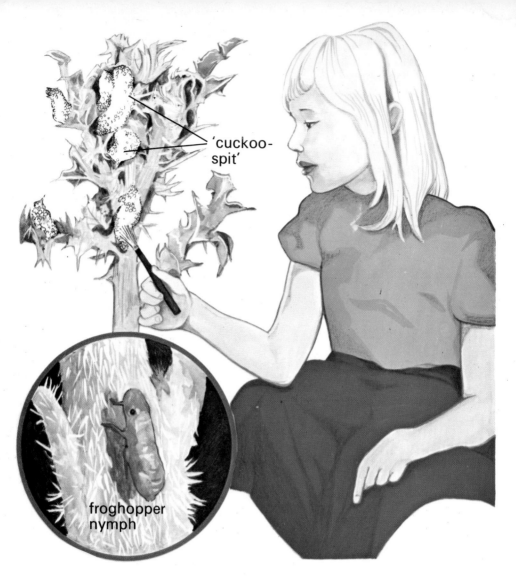

'cuckoo-
spit'

froghopper
nymph

Can you find 'cuckoo-spit' on plants?
It is often on thistles and grasses.
Push away the froth.
See the baby froghopper inside.

10

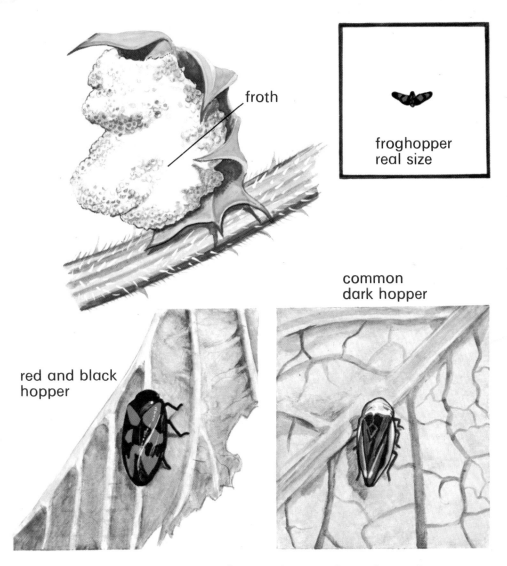

froth

froghopper
real size

common
dark hopper

red and black
hopper

It sucks sap from the plant for food.
It makes the froth for protection.
Look for grown-up froghoppers
as well as young ones.

11

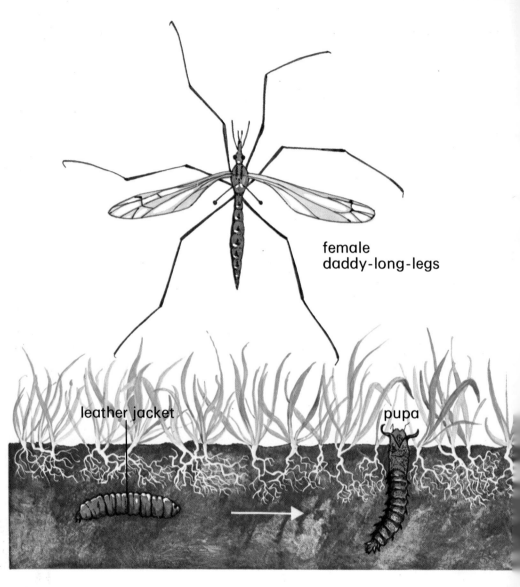

female
daddy-long-legs

leather jacket

pupa

Look for daddy-long-legs in late summer.
They have very thin legs and two wings.
The female lays eggs among the grass roots.

12

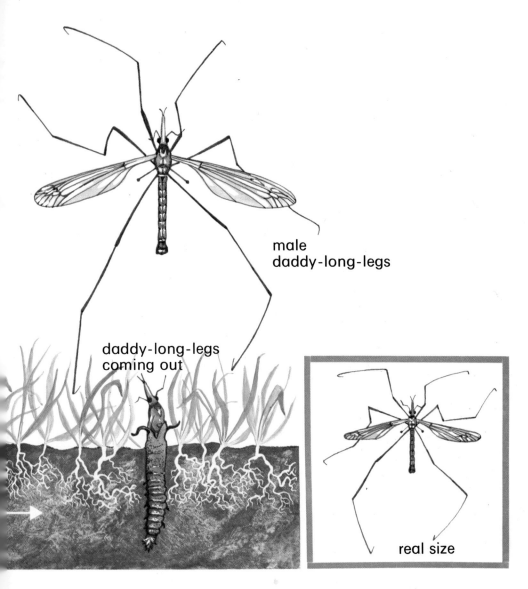

male
daddy-long-legs

daddy-long-legs
coming out

real size

The larva is called a leather-jacket.
It eats grass roots all winter.
In spring it changes to a pupa.

13

common 7-spot ladybird

10-spot ladybird

22-spot ladybird

6-spot ladybird

2-spot ladybird

eyed ladybird

Ladybirds are brightly-coloured beetles.
Look for them in spring and summer.
Count the spots.

14

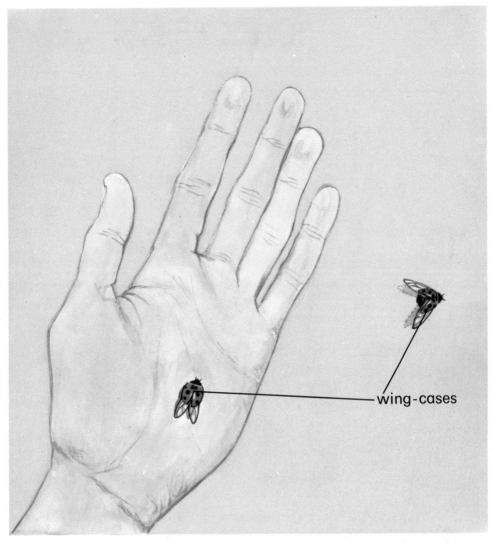

wing-cases

Let a ladybird crawl on your hand.
Soon the outside wing-cases will open.
The flying wings will unfold.
Watch the ladybird fly.

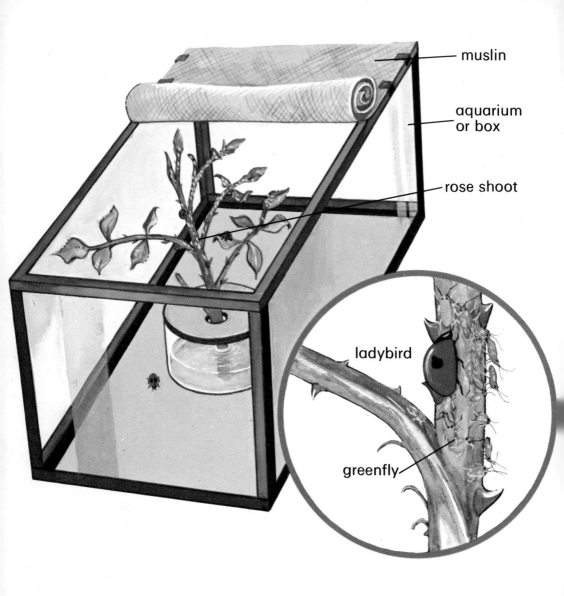

muslin

aquarium or box

rose shoot

ladybird

greenfly

It is easy to keep a few ladybirds.
They eat greenflies.
Give them more every day.
16

cardinal
beetle

rose chafer

two-coloured
leaf beetle

soldier
beetle

Here are pictures
of more pretty beetles to look for.

dahlia

earwig

Earwigs like to press themselves
into corners.
You can often shake them out
from between flower petals.
18

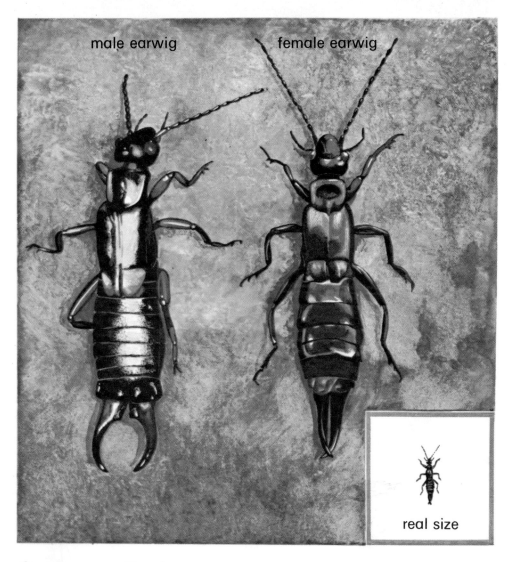

male earwig female earwig

real size

Can you find
some male and female earwigs?
Earwigs do have small wings,
but they never fly.

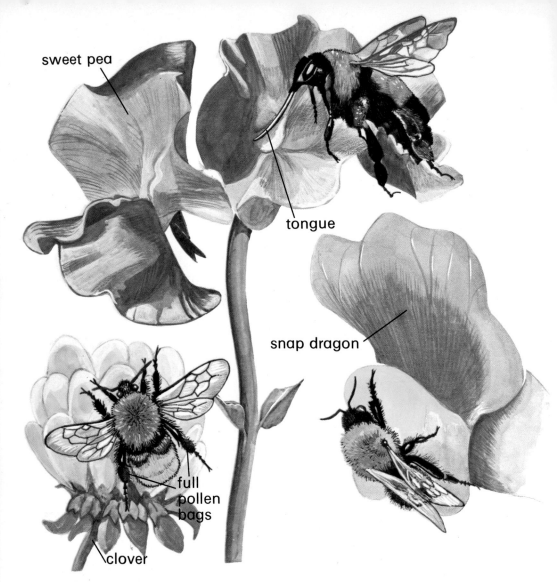

sweet pea

tongue

snap dragon

full
pollen
bags

clover

Watch bumble bees on the flowers
in summer.
They are looking for food.
Can you see where they carry pollen?

20

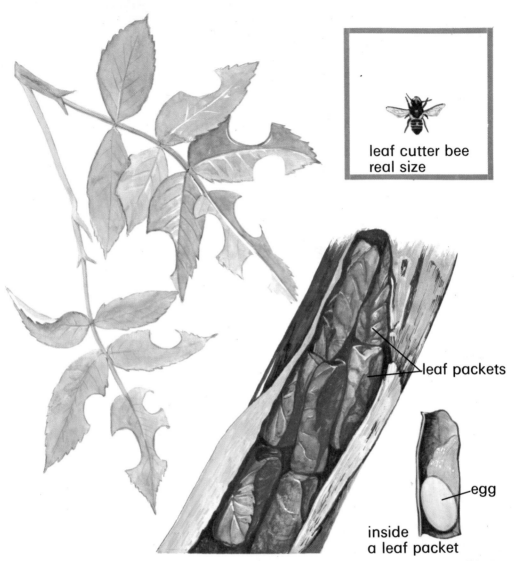

leaf cutter bee
real size

leaf packets

egg

inside
a leaf packet

Have you seen leaves with holes like these?
The leaf cutter bee makes them.
See how the bee uses the pieces of leaf
to wrap its egg.

21

Wasps are busy in summer.
Try to see what they eat.
If you do not touch them,
they won't sting you.

22

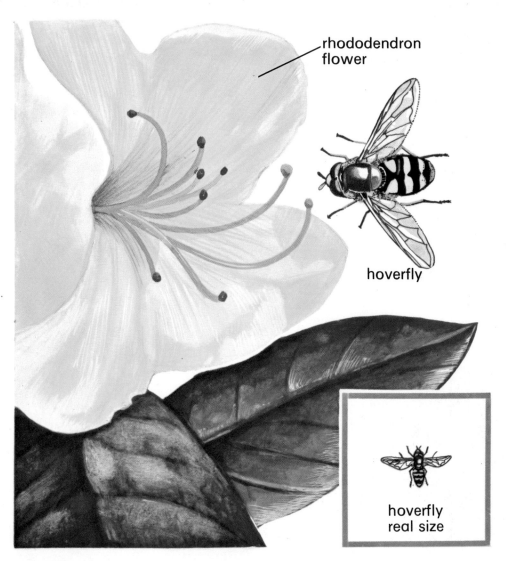

rhododendron
flower

hoverfly

hoverfly
real size

A hoverfly looks like a wasp,
but it only has two wings and no sting.
It hovers in the air near flowers.
It feeds on nectar.

23

ant hill

Many ants live together.
Some live in soil.
Some live under stones.
Some make a heap of twigs and stems.

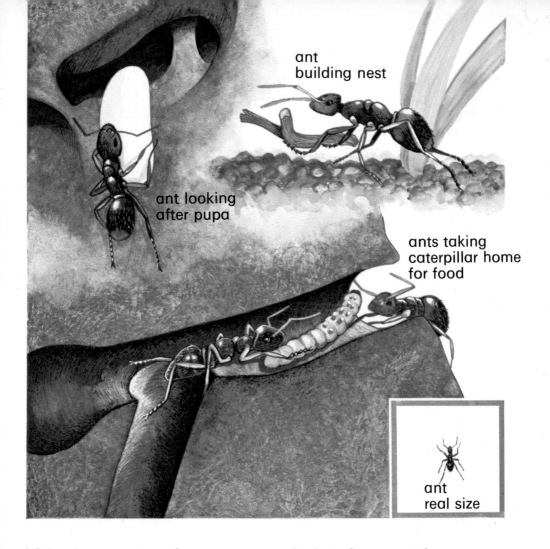

ant
building nest

ant looking
after pupa

ants taking
caterpillar home
for food

ant
real size

Worker ants have special jobs to do.
Some collect food. Others build the nest.
Some are guards.
Some look after the eggs, larvae,
and pupae.

25

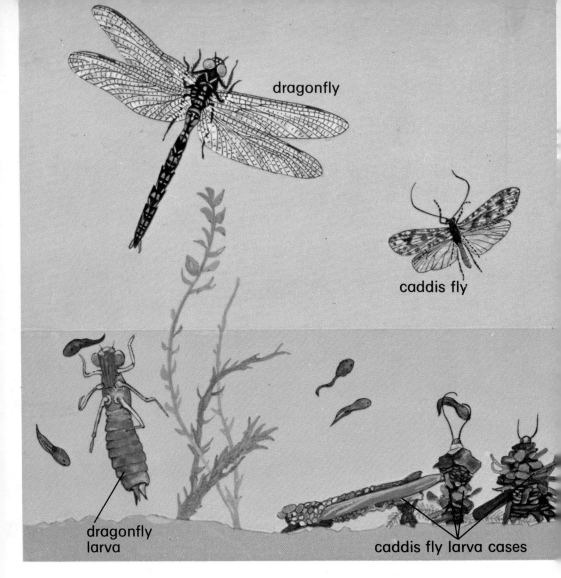

dragonfly

caddis fly

dragonfly
larva

caddis fly larva cases

These insects spend part of their life
in water.
The caddis larva makes a case for itself.
The caddis fly comes out of this.

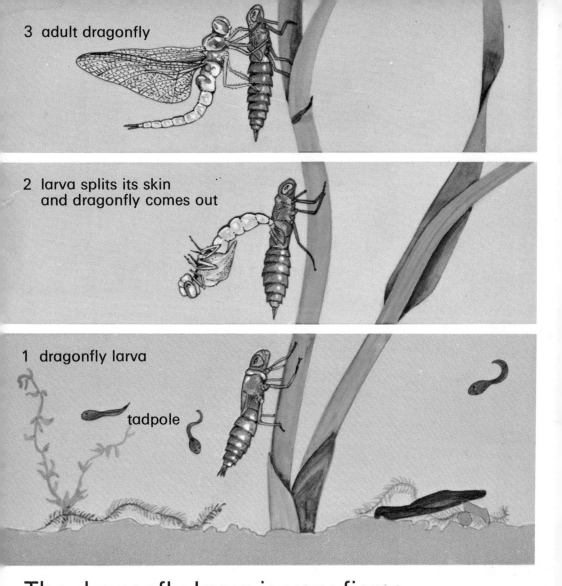

3 adult dragonfly

2 larva splits its skin
  and dragonfly comes out

1 dragonfly larva

tadpole

The dragonfly larva is very fierce.
It eats many tadpoles.
The grown larva crawls up a stem.
The skin splits and out comes a dragonfly.

27

Index

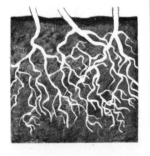